EARLY ROAD LOCATION [VIRGINIA]: KEY TO DISCOVERING HISTORIC RESOURCES?

Virginia Genealogical Society
Richmond, Virginia

Published With Permission from the

Virginia Transportation Research Council
(A Cooperative Organization Sponsored Jointly by the Virginia
Department of Transportation and
the University of Virginia)

HERITAGE BOOKS
2008

HERITAGE BOOKS

AN IMPRINT OF HERITAGE BOOKS, INC.

Books, CDs, and more—Worldwide

For our listing of thousands of titles see our website
at
www.HeritageBooks.com

Published 2008 by
HERITAGE BOOKS, INC.
Publishing Division
100 Railroad Avenue #104
Westminster, Maryland 21157

International Standard Book Number: 978-0-7884-3368-9

Trace of the early 18C Buck Mountain Road,
Albemarle County, Virginia.

ABSTRACT

Early Road Location: The Key to Discovering Historic Resources?

The paper describes a unique methodology used in surveying and documenting architecture along eighteenth century road systems in Virginia which could be used as a prototype in other areas. In the method described the historian, geographer, and architectural historian collaborate in research in primary sources, such as court records, as well as secondary ones, including surveying and documenting the formal and vernacular architecture associated with such an early road system up to the twentieth century. Since it includes course work in the School of Architecture at the University of Virginia, it provides the student with a learning experience in interrelated disciplines outside the classroom and an introduction to the architectural patterns associated with an early road system as opposed to the usual town setting context.

The paper also describes the origin of the collaboration, the early roads surveyed, the road order abstract methodology, the architectural survey course methodology and the results, future studies, and some of the developing applications of the process.

EARLY ROAD LOCATION: THE KEY TO DISCOVERING HISTORIC RESOURCES?

by

Nathaniel Mason Pawlett
Faculty Research Historian

and

K. Edward Lay
Assistant Dean
School of Architecture
University of Virginia

INTRODUCTION

The Virginia Highway & Transportation Research Council's research in the history of Virginian roads has demonstrated that today's basic road network in Albemarle County was laid down within 25 years of the threshold of settlement, which occurred about 1725 for this part of the Virginian Piedmont. This principle is extensible to the rest of Virginia where the basic road network survives in place today, overlaid with the two-and four-lane highways constructed from the 1920's onward. With the era of interstate construction now rapidly drawing to a close, it would seem that most of the new construction, as well as reconstruction, will soon be taking place within the corridors of these early roads along routes now at least several hundred years old in most places. Some method of inventorying historic structures and sites along these routes is, therefore, needed to satisfy present and future environmental requirements as the rationalization and upgrading of these roads continue. Beginning in 1976, just such a method was jointly developed by the School of Architecture at the University of Virginia and the Council.

Studies conducted with this method can serve many uses. Besides their obvious importance in terms of history and architecture, they can be used in making decisions regarding planning by federal, state, and local historic and preservation bodies, and architectural review boards. They can aid greatly in decisions as to just what is worthy of preservation and restoration, where architectural design control districts might be designated, where industry should be located, and, perhaps most importantly of all since they are road-related studies, where future highway improvements should be located for minimum adverse impact on important historical features.

If, as has so often been said, history is really the story of roads and the events which occurred along them, then architectural history can be said to consist to a great extent of the study of the buildings to be found along those same roads. In the past, architectural historians have documented individual buildings with little regard to their context area or, at most, have investigated buildings in a community or town setting. Recently, however, the identification of early eighteenth century Virginia roads and their traces has begun to define yet another, unique context area that can provide clues to the architectural patterns associated with it through time.

Architectural surveys along Virginia road systems grew out of a program of research into the history of road and bridge building technology in Virginia initiated in 1972 by the Virginia Highway and Transportation Research Council, a cooperative organization sponsored jointly by the Virginia Department of Highways and Transportation and the University of Virginia.[1] An advisory committee consisting of members from the University of Virginia, the University of West Virginia, the Virginia Historic Landmarks Commission, the Historic American Engineering Record, and the History and Heritage Committee of the American Society of Civil Engineers, as well as people from the affected divisions of the Virginia Department of Highways and Transportation, was formed to guide the work.

Research has progressed along two broad lines: a study of structures and a study of roads. The initial project is a statewide survey of metal truss bridges that has resulted in a series of 7 reports,[2] and the second project deals with the history of roads in Virginia,[3] in which Albemarle County is being used in a pilot study for the years from its earliest origins about 1725 to the coming of the turnpike era in 1816. In the latter project, eight reports in a series entitled "Historic Roads of Virginia" have been issued.

The establishment and maintenance of public roads were important functions of the county court from the colonial period to 1870 in Virginia. Each road was opened and maintained by an overseer or surveyor of the roads charged with this responsibility and appointed by the gentlemen justices. For the purpose, he was usually assigned all the labouring male titheables living on or near the road.

Major projects, such as bridges over rivers, demanding considerable expenditures were executed by commissioners appointed by the court to select the site and contract with workmen for the construction. Where bridges connected two counties, a commission was appointed by each to cooperate in executing the work.

From the foregoing, it can be seen that the road and bridge orders contained in the order books of the counties from which Albemarle ultimately came to be formed were primary sources of information for this study. These were put into typescript and indexed and published by the Council. The ready availability of these road orders in a convenient, printed form greatly facilitated the development of the histories of individual roads and made possible the next step in the evolution of road-oriented architectural surveys.

EARLY ROADS SURVEYED

In December 1974, the Council received a request from James A. Bear, Jr., curator of Monticello, for research assistance in determining the original route of the Three Notch'd Road between Richmond and the Shenandoah Valley.

Of the colonial roads (see Figure 1) constructed during the eighteenth century as settlement moved across Piedmont and Southside Virginia, one of the most significant was this Three Notch'd Road, which ran from Richmond to the Shenandoah Valley as a main east-west route from the 1730's to the 1930's, when it was superseded by U. S. Route 250. Originally an Indian and game path, various sections of it were gradually improved to the status of roads during the 1730's as the settlers moved into the upper Piedmont. Known-originally as the Mountain Road, or Mountain Ridge Road, it derived the name Three Notch'd Road from a system of marks it received after 1742. As early as 1737, it already possessed trees numbered with the miles from 0 to at least 46, running from west to east along its route, as an aid to travelers.

Although the road appears on late eighteenth century maps, it can first be specifically located on the maps prepared by the Confederate Engineers, and these indicate that it remains very nearly on its historic course from Richmond to the Valley.

The report by the Council on this eighteenth century road elicited so much interest that it was expanded and published to include a folding map, an appendix of the pertinent information from the order books of Louisa, Goochland, Albemarle, and Orange Counties, citations in the Virginia Gazette of Williamsburg, and photographs of portions of the road still in service and some of the more significant examples of eighteenth and nineteenth century architecture remaining along it.[4]

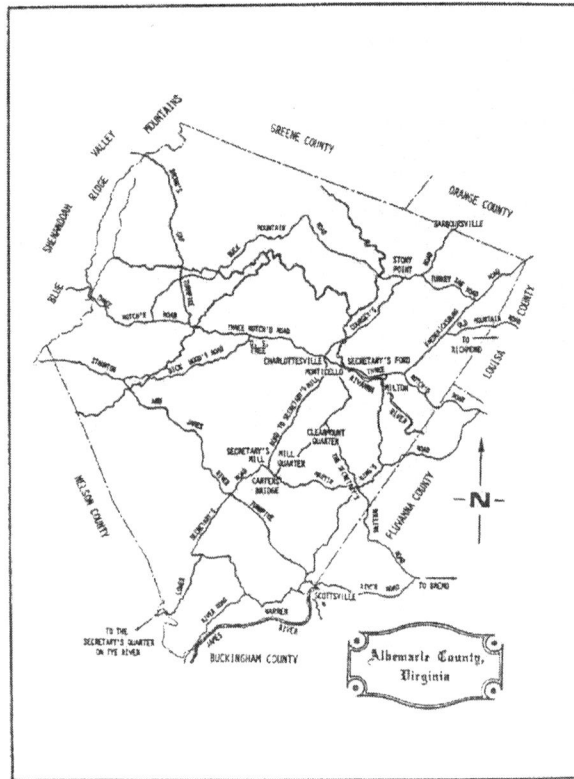

Figure 1. Early roads of Albermarle County.

Convinced of the potential for a very interesting, unique, and innovative course tying architectural development to the existence of the road itself and its subsequent influence on Virginia history, the School of Architecture at the University of Virginia initiated a course entitled "Architectural Patterns Associated with Virginia Road Traces." The initial semester of this course dealt with the surveying and documenting of architecture along the Three Notch'd Road between the Blue Ridge Mountains and the Goochland County line. Following the success of this venture, the course was made permanent. In subsequent semesters, other roads of Albemarle County were surveyed.

Considerably shorter than the Three Notch'd Road, the Buck Mountain Road ran from the modern village of Stony Point across the northern part of present Albemarle County, skirting the foot of the Blue Ridge Mountains. At the time of the creation of the initial portion of the road and until 1761, this area was the westernmost portion of Louisa County and the road then served as the main county road for the area. Although the road was constructed in 1742, the name "Buck Mountain Road" first appears in records in 1747.

4

Despite the Buck Mountain Road's status as the main county road in its area there was no road through the Southwest Mountain to connect the westernmost portion with the rest of Louisa County before 1745. That year, a road was opened through the Turkey Sag (gap) to allow direct communication with the county seat and the ports of Richmond, Newcastle, and Hanovertown. From this time until at least the 1790's, much of the trade of the areas along the Buck Mountain Road, as well as that from the Shenandoah Valley, must have travelled this route to market. Indeed, as late as 1850, tobacco from this area was still following this route to market. After 1790, however, the new town of Milton, at the head of navigation on the Rivanna River several miles east of Charlottesville, became more the focus of the road and its trade. Well located, the essential fabric of this road remains' intact arid in service along its original course after 235 years of use by Virginians.

Another road that has been studied is actually two separate roads built under the auspices of John Carter (1690-1743), secretary of state for Virginia. Carter," although never residing in the Albemarle area, patented in 1730 a tract of 9,350 acres just south of the present Charlottesville. Shortly, he established two quarters on this property - one called Clearmount and the other the Mill - and began to produce tobacco. To provide an outlet for this crop, a road was built about 1734 from Bremo on the James River up the fork between the James and Rivanna Rivers to the secretary's Clearmount Quarter, and thence, passing near Monticello, on to Secretary's Ford on the Rivanna River at the later site of Charlottesville. Variously called the Secretary's Road, the Secretary's Rolling Road, and the Secretary's Old Rolling Road, the name survives in use today, as does the original road over most of its course. Near Bremo are located some very interesting stone road signs (see Figure 2), milestones (see Figure 3), and a spring and wayside (see Figure 4), all erected much later by the noted John Hartwell Cocke of Bremo Plantation during his service as overseer of roads in the 1820's.

In the early 1740's, another road, also called the Secretary's Road, was opened from the Mill Quarter near Carter's Bridge to the southwestward, terminating at the secretary's other Quarter in the present Amherst-Nelson County area on the Piney River. Although there seems little question as to the use "of the eastern road for tobacco rolling, the principal use of this lower road seems more likely to have been for moving slaves, stock, and tools between the already developed and operating plantations near Carter's Bridge and that located on the new 10,000-acre patent on the Piney River as it was being cleared and made operational.
Most of this lower road also remains in service today as country road.

Figure 2. Stone road sign
near Bremo,
Fluvanna County,
Va., early 19C.

Figure 3. Stone milestone
near Bremo,
Fluvanna County,
Va., early 19C.

Figure 4. Stone spring and wayside, Bremo, Fluvanna Count
Virginia, early 19C.

6

More recently five other eighteenth century roads have been surveyed. Two of these, the Fredericksburg Road and Coursey's Road, probably date from the early 1730's, although their existence has not yet been documented prior to 1742, when surviving records for that area commence. As the Three Notch'd Road was the principal artery connecting the area with the port of Richmond and the capital at Williamsburg, so the Fredickburg Road was in regard to that port town. Coursey's Road served to a lesser degree a somewhat similar function for those living in the area beyond the Southwest Mountain in years immediately following the settlement.

Dick Wood's Road can be dated to 1741 from surviving road orders, although it achieved its present name only late in the century. Leaving the Three Notch'd Road at the D.S. Tree just west of the later site of Charlottesville, it connected with Rockfish Gap in the Blue Ridge besides providing a better route to Richmond for people living in the Rockfish Valley.

The Staunton and James River Turnpike is actually a product of the nineteenth century turnpike era, but the road along this route had its genesis about 1790 and was related to the activities of Wilson Cary Nicholas in promoting his town of Warren on the James River west of the town of Scottsville. Engaged in flour milling on a large scale, Nicholas required Valley wheat to feed his _ills and distillery there, and a more convenient road connection than then existed would ensure this besides serving to further the town as a river port and the Valley's connection with the east. This road was created by using portions of existing roads and cutting some additional sections to rationalize the route in a few places. Styled "the new-cut road to Warren" in a number of early road orders, its eastern terminus finally became Scottsville, and a turnpike company was formed to improve and maintain the road from Staunton in the Valley to the James River.

Although it is first mentioned in a road order of 1740, the Secretary's Mill was probably constructed about 1735 as a necessary adjunct to Carter's tobacco-planting activities in the area. Of considerable importance to the earliest settlers since few grist mills had yet been constructed in the area, it was located near a strategic road intersection and the gap by which the Hardware River passes through Carter's Mountain. Although the main north-south road (now Route 20) was probably not built specifically for access to this mill, it soon acquired the name of "the road to the late Secretary's Mill" and later the road to "Carter's Mill" or "Carter's Bridge". It first appears under the former name in a road order of 16 August 1746 Old Style, but was probably contemporary with the mill's construction since it ran for perhaps half its length through the Secretary's property.

METHODOLOGY FOR ABSTRACTING ROAD ORDERS

All of the extant road orders in the order books of the counties from which Albemarle developed during the years 1725-1816 were extracted, indexed, and printed by the Virginia Highway & Transportation Research Council during research for the Albemarle road history. The availability of these publications greatly facilitated the later work of those conducting the architectural surveys. All of the county court order books from which the road orders came were in manuscript, often damaged and faded so as to be nearly indecipherable. Then too, most of the early eighteenth century materials (see Figure 5) were in the rather ornate, engrossing script and copperplate of the time, with the phonetic spellings of this period serving to further complicate matters for the researcher.

Nevertheless, a system was devised to enable the researcher to render these road orders literatim into a hand-held tape recorder. Following this, the orders were put into typescript by secretaries who had to set aside some of the modern rules of spelling and learn to render the orders exactly as recorded. Following this transcription, the tapes were compared with the transcripts by the original recorder and errors corrected. After being placed in their final form, the road orders were indexed and published by the Council. In this form the road orders were well-received by a wide variety of organizations and individuals engaged in historical and genealogical research, as well as sociologists, folklorists, and people in a variety of other disciplines.

With these available, it was then possible to produce chronological chains of road orders illustrating the development of the early roads from the threshold of settlement through the eighteenth century. Immediate corroboration for these chains of early road orders was provided by the fact that each of the roads studied had survived under its eighteenth century name down to the time when the Confederate Engineers produced the first detailed maps (see Figure 6) of the counties of Virginia in 1863 and 1864. Most of these roads remain nearly on their original routes.

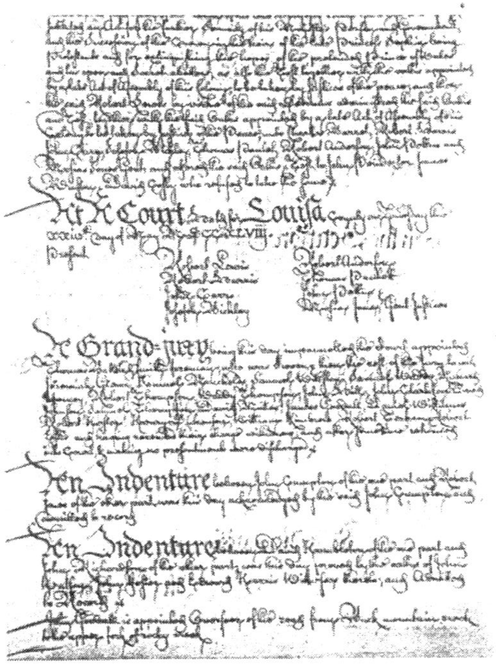

Figure 6. Confederate engineers
map of Albemarle County,
Virginia, c. 1864.

Figure 5. Virginia road order from
18C Order Book.

METHODOLOGY USED IN ARCHITECTURAL SURVEY COURSE

The architectural surveys project at the University of Virginia is a three semester hour credit elective course open to all graduate and undergraduate students in the School of Architecture. The only prerequisites are access to an automobile and a 35mm SLR camera.

Teams of two or three students survey and document the formal and vernacular architecture associated with a segment of an eighteenth century road, including buildings erected up to the Civil War or perhaps the turn of the century. Only those extant buildings whose access originally emanated from the road are included. At least fifteen buildings per team member along at least eight miles of road are surveyed in one semester.

The survey consists of identifying and photographing the associated architecture and recording architectural data and historical information from such secondary sources as the present and previous owners, local historians, newspaper articles, real estate brochures, and local histories. Documentation consists of primary source research through county record searches of deeds, wills, inventories, plats, tax lists, and insurance records (for example, those of the Mutual Assurance Society and the Sanborn Insurance Company).

Research begins with a review of early maps showing major landowners, using an 1864 Confederate Engineers' map, the 1875 Peyton map, and the 1907 Massie map, all of Albemarle County, in which the University of Virginia is located. Turn of the century mail route maps and the 1930's state soil maps also indicate building locations. Next, aerial photographs and United States or U. S. Geological Survey 7.5 minute topographic maps are reviewed. Research in the local histories and the files of the Virginia Historic Landmarks Commission often reveals much secondary source material. This is followed by actually traversing the road and noting, from a windshield survey, all buildings that appear to have been built prior to 1900.

Thereafter, an average of about three buildings are field surveyed in an afternoon. One surveyor talks with the owner and records any historical or architectural information that might be known, while the other photographs, makes a written architectural description, notes the compass direction of the main door orientation, sketches a first floor plan, and measures the outside with a tape measure or by stepping off the exterior. Where applicable, the brick bonding pattern and the absence of a ridge board are always noted as a quick field technique for approximating the date of construction. Photographs usually include two of the exterior from opposite compass directions in order to get all four elevations, sometimes a straight-on elevation, which includes a range pole to graphically portray feet and inches on the photograph (see Figure 7), interior mantels (see Figure 8) and stairways, and significant details of construction, doors, windows, and moldings. Each building owner is queried for information pertaining to other eighteenth and nineteenth century buildings in the area and about older local persons knowledgeable about buildings. It is often helpful to have them call ahead to their next neighbor to inform him that the survey team is coming. Cultivating the crowd at the general store is also advantageous. Most property owners are very receptive; each team member is, however, given a letter of introduction that includes a telephone number at the School of Architecture to call in case any questions arise.

The end result is a report which is bound and catalogued and placed in the Fiske Kimball Fine Arts Library at the University.[5] Included are survey sheets and photographs on each building arranged sequentially along the road. Each book is catalogued so that each road has a series number permitting more volumes to be added as additional portions of the road are surveyed.

The survey sheet (see Figures 9 and 10) includes the name and location of the building using the Universal Transverse Mercator location system, the style and date of construction, the original and present use of the building, the original and present owners, the names of the surveyors and the date of the field survey, the historical and architectural descriptions, the main floor plan (see Figure 11), and the sources of information. Since dwellings make up the majority of the buildings, all other building types - such as taverns, churches, schools, mills, depots, and stores - are depicted on one 20.3cm. x 25.4cm. (8 inch x 10 inch) dry-mounted photograph (see Figure 10) facing the survey sheet, while dwellings have two 12.7cm. x 17.8cm. (5 inch x 7 inch) ones (see Figure 9) to a page. All additional photographs, such as those of other elevations, outbuildings, mantels, stairways, and details, on anyone building complex are mounted on the back of the photograph sheet in 7.6cm. x 12.7cm. (3 inch x 5 inch) format see Figure 12). A U. S. Geological Survey topographic map (see Figure 13) folded and placed in the back of the book locates the surveyed road in yellow and other eighteenth century roads that intersect this one with a dashed red line. The map has blue arrows pointing to houses, red arrows to building types other than houses, and a smaller yellow arrow indicating the direction the building's main entrance door faces, giving building orientation.

Figure 8. Mantel detail, Snow Hill, Surry County, Va.

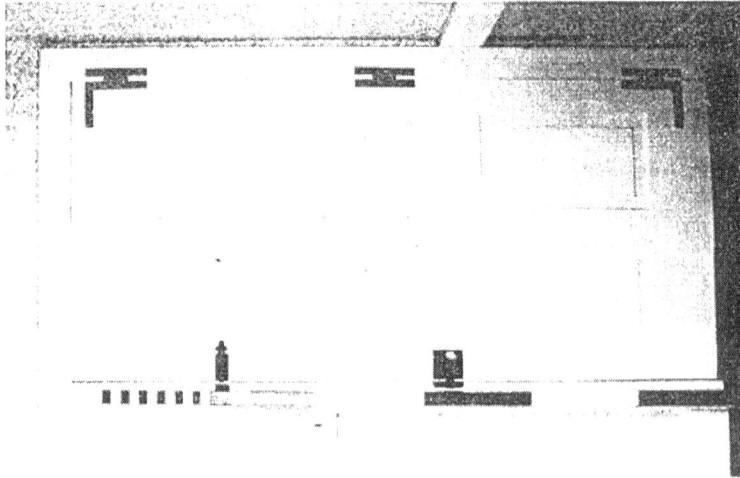

Figure 7. Photograph using graphic scale, Morven Cottage, Albermarle County, Va.

12

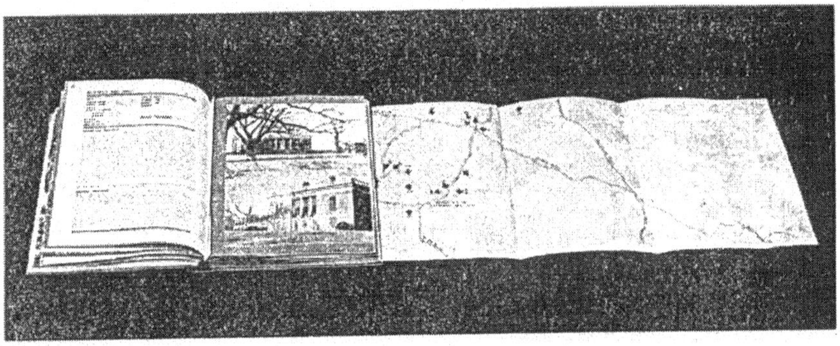

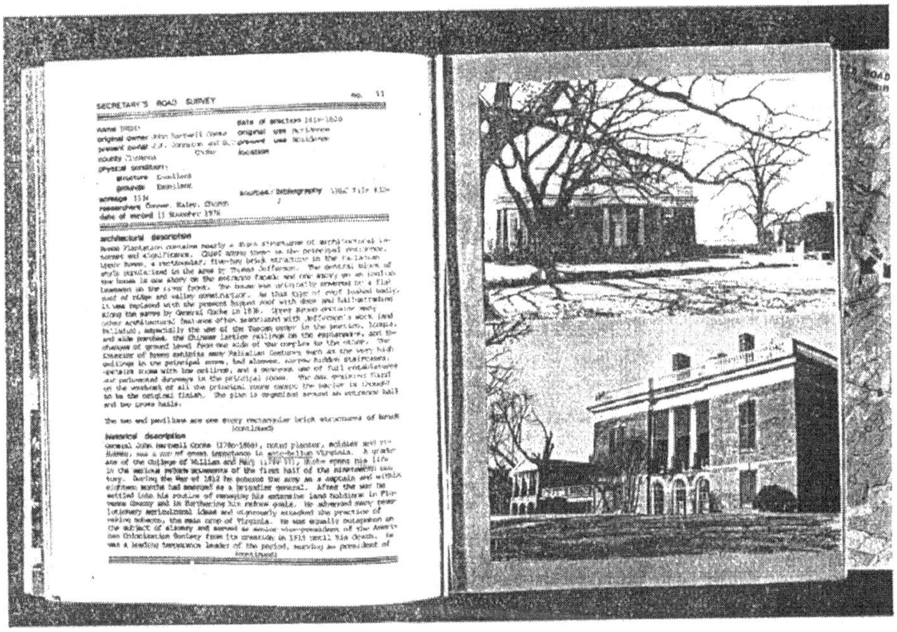

Figure 9. Bremo, Fluvanna County, Virginia, 1818-1820.

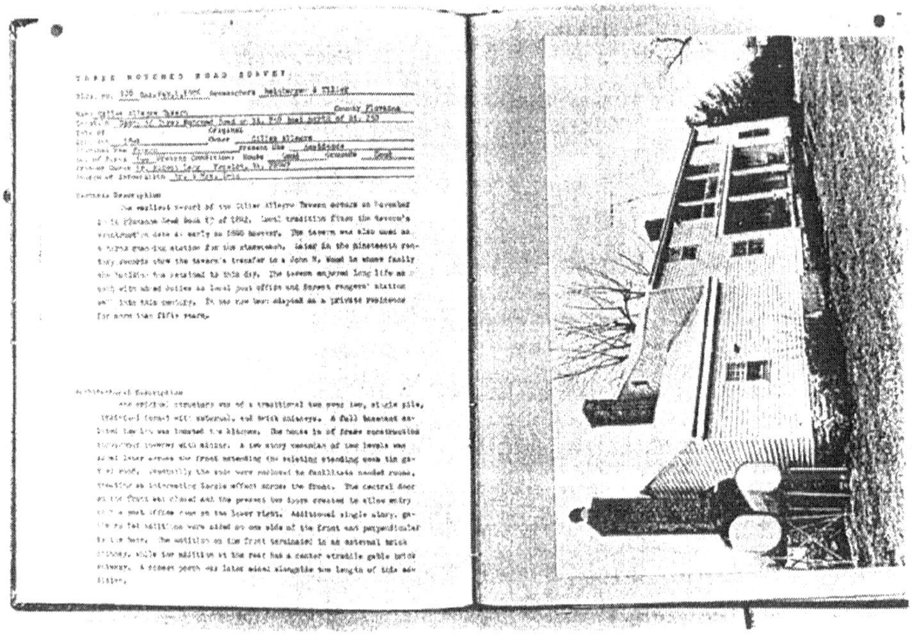

Figure 10. Giles Allegre's Tavern, Fluvanna County, Virginia, 1841.

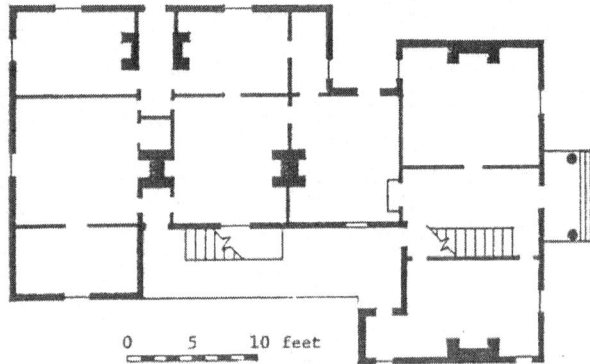

Ashlawn

Figure 11. Floor plan example, Ash Lawn (James
Monroe House), Albemarle County,
Virginia, c. 1799.

Figure 12. Sunnyfields, Albemarle Co., Virginia,
c. 1830-1840.

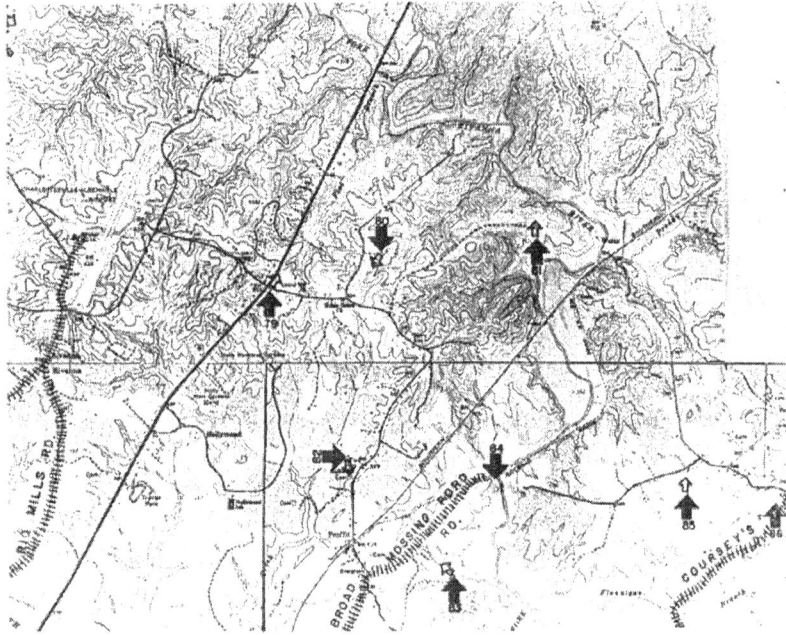

Figure 13.   Example of notations on U.S.G.S. topographic map.

Other information included is a chronological abstract of data pertaining to this road from the county road orders (see Appendix A), a history of the road (see Appendix B), plats from the county survey books showing the road location (see Figure 14), and a comparative statement pertaining to any architectural patterns that seem to emerge (see Appendix C). In addition, photographs of the road trace (as illustrated in the frontispiece of this report), old mileage markers, old road signs, old survey markers (see Figure 15), and the gravestone of the original owner (see Figure 16) are often included. Detailed studies of some buildings are completed in conjunction with the Historic American Buildings Survey where actual measured drawings (see Figure 17) are made, as they were for this endangered house.

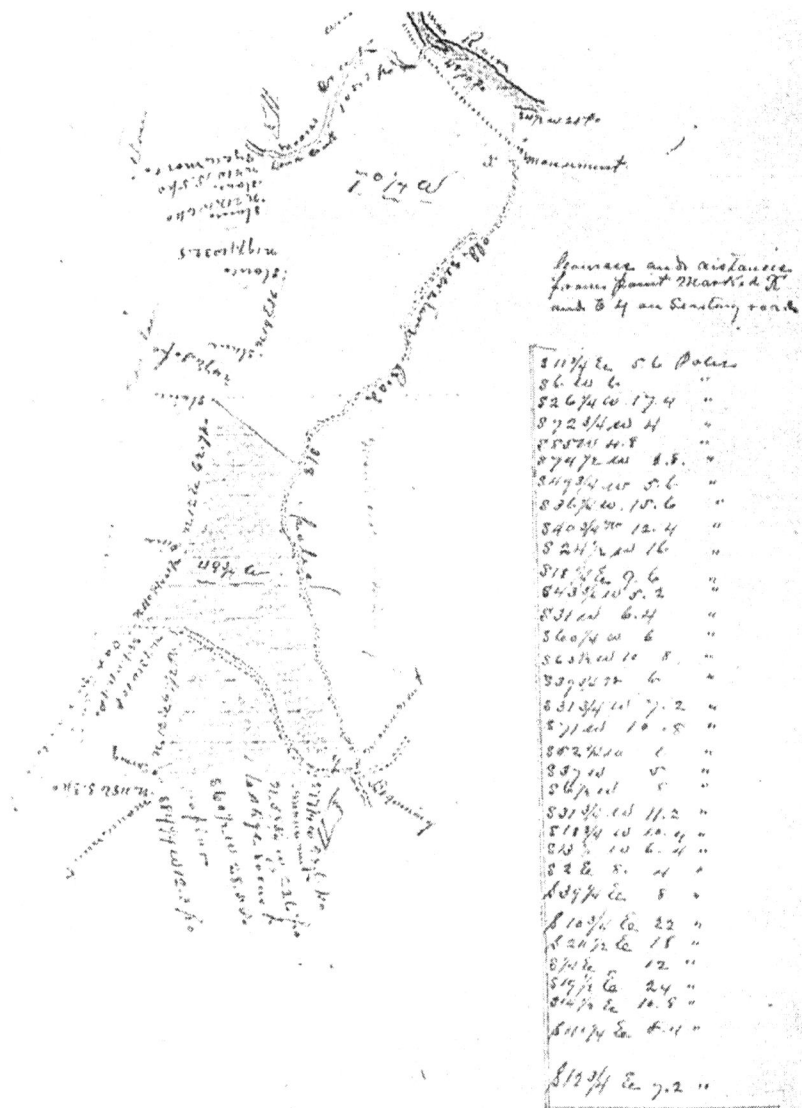

Figure 14. Albermarle County plat showing road location
along Secretary's Road near Monticello
(D.B. 93-316, 1887).

17

Figure 16. Gravestone of original property owner.

Figure 15. Survey marker along Three Notch'd Road.

18

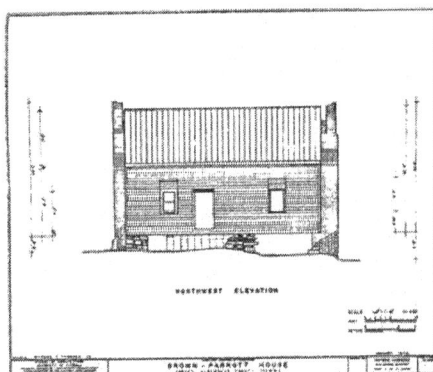

Figure 17. LAY/PAWLETT HABS Measured Drawing of Brown-Parrott House, Albemarle County, Va., C. 1780. (Richard Thomsen)

RESULTS, FUTURE STUDIES AND APPLICATIONS

During the first two years of the course (1976 and 1977), more than 300 buildings along three early eighteenth century roads - the Three Notch'd Road, the Buck Mountain Road, and the Secretary's Road - were identified, documented, and catalogued in twelve bound volumes in the Fiske Kimball Fine Arts Library at the University (see Appendix D). Since then, portions of five other eighteenth century roads - the Fredericksburg Road, Coursey's Road, Dick Wood's Road, the Staunton & James River Turnpike, and the road to the Secretary's Mill have been surveyed. Thus far, more than 200 additional buildings have been identified from these studies and described in thirteen more volumes.

Because of the travel distances involved, Albemarle County's early roads are being surveyed first. Of the significant early roads in Albemarle, there remain the River Road, Martin King's Road, and the Brown's Gap Turnpike. Many of the same early roads can be followed into and through the adjacent counties to their destinations and the architecture along their routes surveyed. This procedure has already been followed in the case of the Three Notch'd Road, and this work is now substantially complete through the counties of Louisa and Fluvanna into Goochland County. Besides those in Albemarle, a multitude of other documentable early road systems located within easy driving distance remain to be investigated.

19

From the foregoing it can readily be seen that sufficient information is already on hand to allow consideration of questions of the significance of architectural patterns and similarities along the roads and their relationship to the early flow of settlement, social and economic structure, and geography and soil types. Some exploratory essays have already been written. More will doubtless emerge as the course continues and the accumulation of information over ever wider areas enables beginning a consideration of some of the larger issues involved. Some of the longer coherent roads running from Tidewater Virginia to the Blue Ridge should produce examples of architectural development dating from perhaps the 1680's to 1800 and covering the whole period of the settlement of Piedmont Virginia. Sufficient distinct similarities in style, form, and use of materials should be visible in the surviving buildings along these roads to provide an insight into the evolution of form, the migration of building types, and the acculturation in the material culture between different ethnic groups.

The course itself has already inspired emulation by Glassboro College in New Jersey (under the direction of Herbert A. Richardson). Beyond this, the course has resulted in the production of a number of useful studies of extremely high quality. Not only is the work itself of a high quality, it has been achieved with a minimal expenditure of governmental funds while simultaneously providing a significant learning experience for a host of budding architectural historians and preservationists.

Besides the original reports on these studies, bound and placed on deposit at the Fiske Kimball Fine Arts Library at the University, copies are regularly provided to the Virginia Historic Landmarks Commission and to the Environmental Quality Division of the Virginia Department of Highways & Transportation at Richmond. The potential for the utilization of these documents in the planning process by other agencies also exists and will doubtless soon be examined.

Some intimations of the future drawn from the past:

Albemarle County, formed in 1744 from Goochland, had its basic road network laid down between 1725 and 1750. With additions and improvements, the principal part of this network remains in service today and still constitutes most of the important roads of the county. Along it has flowed, and still flows, the economic, social and political life of the community. It is this skeleton along which are arranged most of the plantations, mills, battlefields and significant historical and archaeological sites, ranging from Monticello to the Indians' soapstone quarries near Alberene.

All of this continues to feed a growing suspicion that
there is a great coincidence of animal path, Indian path,
colonial road, turnpike and modern highway down through the
years. If this is so, then early road locations may also serve
to provide clews to archaeologists looking for Indian sites.
Beyond the narrower compass of the road course itself, other
researchers are exploring the possibility of using these data in
the computer mapping of historic sites to be used in the
planning process and, ultimately, in the development of a
predictive capability which may allow the early identification
of sensitive zones in the
path of development.

Today everyone would recognize the Michie Tavern (see
Figure 18) of about 1765 as a historically significant
structure, but how many would recognize the woebegone little
Brooking House (see Figure 19) on the Three Notch'd Road as one.
Yet in the first quarter of this century the Michie Tavern stood
derelict alongside the Buck Mountain Road looking not much
better than the Brooking House does today. Surely history is the
story of roads, and architectural history the story of the
buildings along them. Both are worthy of preservation.

Figure 18.   Michie Tavern, Albemarle County, Virginia,
             1750-1780.

Figure 19.   Brooking House, Goochland County, Virginia ca.
             1800.

22

REFERENCES

1. See Howard Newlon, Jr., <u>A Proposal For Initiating Research on History of Road and Bridge Building Technology in Virginia.</u> Charlottesville, Virginia Highway & Transportation Research Council, December 1972.)

2. See Dan Grove Deibler, <u>Metal Truss Bridges in Virginia: 1865-1932.</u>

   I. <u>An Examination of the Development of the Truss Form Along With An Annotated List of Nineteenth and Early Twentieth Century Bridge Companies</u>, (Charlottesville, Virginia Highway & Transportation Research Council, May 1975).

   II. <u>The Staunton Construction District,</u> Charlottesville, Virginia Highway & Transportation Research Council, May 1975).

   III. <u>The Culpeper Construction District,</u> Charlottesville, Virginia Highway & Transportation Research Council, December 1975).

   IV. <u>The Fredericksburg Construction District,</u> Charlottesville, Virginia Highway & Transportation Research Council, May 1976).

   V. <u>The Richmond.Construction District,</u> (Charlottesville, Virginia Highway & Transportation Research Council, June 1976).

   Paula A. C. Spero, <u>Metal Truss Bridges <i>in</i> Virginia: 1865-1932.</u>

   VI. <u>The Lynchburg Construction District,</u> (Charlottesville, Virginia Highway & Transportation Research Council, November 1979).

Howard Newlon, Jr., <u>Criteria For Preservation and Adaptive Use of Historic Highway Structures</u>: Interim Report No.1: A Trial Rating System for Truss Bridges, (Charlottesville, Virginia Highway & Transportation Research Council, January 1978).

The initial project, begun by Dan G. Deibler, resulted in five reports. This continues under Paula A. C. Spero. The criteria for preservation were formulated by Deibler and Howard Newlon and set out in <u>Criteria For Preservation and Adaptive Use of Historic Highway Structures</u>.

23

3. See Nathaniel Mason Pawlett, Preparation of County Road Histories: A Methodology Pilot Study -"Albermarle County Virginia, (Charlottesville, Virginia Highway & Transportation Research Council, January 1974). Begun in 1973 by Pawlett under whose direction have resulted eight reports in a series entitled "Historic Roads of Virginia".

    I. Louisa County Road Orders 1742-1748, (Charlottesville, Virginia Highway & Transportation Research Council, April 1975, revised January 1979).

    II. Goochland County Road Orders 1728-1744, (Charlottesville, Virginia Highway & Transportation Research Council, June 1975, revised April 1979).

    III. Albemarle County Road Orders 1744-1748, (Charlottesville, Virginia Highway & Transportation Research Council, June 1975, revised June 1979).

    IV. The Route of the Three Notch'd Road: A Preliminary Report, with Howard Newlon, (Charlottesville, Virginia Highway & Transportation Research Council, January 1976).

    V. An Index to Roads in the Albemarle County Surveyors Books 1744-1853, (Charlottesville, Virginia Highway & Transportation Research Council, March 1976).

    VI. A Brief History of the Staunton and James River Turnpike, by Douglas Young, (Charlottesville, Virginia Highway & Transportation Research Council, May 1976, revised August 1976).

    VII. Albemarle County Road Orders 1783-1816, (Charlottesville, Virginia Highway & Transportation Research Council, December 1975, revised May 1980).

    VIII. A Brief History of the Roads of Virginia 1607-1840, (Charlottesville, Virginia Highway & Transportation Research Council, October 1977).

    IX. A Guide to the Preparation of County Road Histories, (Charlottesville, Virginia Highway & Transportation Research Council, March 1979).

4. Nathaniel Mason Pawlett, with Howard Newlon, Jr., The Route of The Three Notch'd Road: A Preliminary Report, Charlottesville, Virginia Highway & Transportation Research Council, 1976).

5. See K. Edward Lay, <u>Architecture Associated With Virginia Road Traces,</u> (VRT) Series. Bound Volumes of this series are catalogued in the Fiske Kimball Fine Arts Library at the University of Virginia.

    VRT-1   The Three Notch'd Road in Virginia

          Vol. 1,2 by Guy M. Lapsley and Richard P. Thomsen, Jr.
          Vol. 3 by Tracy S. Scharer
          Vol. 4, 5 by Mark E. Reinberger and De Teel P. Tiller
          Vol. 6 by Karen Lang Kummer

    VRT-2   The Buck Mountain Road in Virginia

          Vol. 1,2 by Cynthia Ann Macleod and Mark James Wenger
          Vol. 3 by Lori Feldman, Margaret Pearson Mickler, and Marin Perdue

    VRT-3   The Secretary's Road in Virginia

          Vol. 1, 2 by Barbara Hume Church, Michael Francis Conner, and Drucilla Gatewood Haley
          Vol. 3,4 by David Allan Edwards, Mark Randolph Wenger, and George Humphrey Yetter

    VRT-4   The Fredericksburg Road in Virginia

          Vol. 1,2 by Ann L. Brush and A. James Siracuse
          Vol. 3,4 by Ann L. Brush

    VRT-5   The Staunton & James River Turnpike in Virginia

          Vol. 1,2,3 by Margaret G. Davis, Ann R. Fair, Kathryn M. Kuranda and Stuart N. Siegel

    VRT-6   Coursey's Road in Virginia

          Vol. 1, 2 by M. Ward Hill and Patricia A. Murphy

    VRT-7   Dick Wood's Road in Virginia

          Vol. 1,2 by Charles Rhinelander

    VRT-8   Road to Secretary's Mill in Virginia

          Vol. 1 by E. Claire Welch

APPENDIX A

Abstract Pertaining to the Road from the County Order Books

SELECTED ROAD ORDERS PERTAINING TO THE SECRATARY'S ROAD

Goochland County Road Orders: 1728-1744

16 July 1734 O.S., p. 273
Road to be cleared.
Ordered a road to be cleared from the Round Pond Road to Col1[?]
John Carter's Plantation where Robert Davis is Overseer and
Charles Lynch is appointed Surveyor of the said Road./.

21 January 1734 O.S., p. 314
Road not to be esteemed publick.
Ordered that the Road from the Round Pond to the Secretary's
Quarter be esteemed no Publick Road./.

19 September 1738 O.S., p. 358
Road to be cleared.
On the Pet. of Robert Davis leave is granted him to clear a Road
from the Secretary's land on the mountains of the North River to
his new Settlement on Tye River.

17 March 1740 O.S., p. 596
Road to be cleared.
Ordered that the road be cleared from the Secretary's mill to
the lower main road to the Manacan Town ferry and that Chas
Jordan be Surveyor thereof. Ordered that Wamachs gang do assist
in opening the said road.

15 September 1741 O.S., p.3
Road to be cleared.
On the petition of David Lewis, George Taylor, William Hargis,
Samuel Stiles, James ffidler, Hugh ffrazier, Howard Cash, James
Treland, David Lewis, Junr, Chas Caffry David Rees, William
Lewis, Abraham Slaten, & William Williams. Leave is granted them
to clear a road from the Secretary's fford to the D.S. tree. And
that the petitioners be exempt from working on any other road.

20 September 1743 O.S., p. 274
Surveyors of Roads.
David Lewis is appointed Surveyor of the Road from the D.S. tree
down to Moors Creek and into the Secretary's Road and that the
Tithables near the said road do clear the same.

APPENDIX B

Example of the History of the Road

THE TRACE OF THE SECRETARY'S ROAD

On 16 July 1734 (O.S.), the Justices of the Goochland County Court ordered that a road be cleared from the Round Pond Road to John Carter's plantation.[1] This property was located in present-day Albemarle County, Virginia, and was owned by John Carter, Secretary of the Council of the Colony of Virginia. Carter, son of Robert (King) Carter of Corrotoman, had a large land holding near Carter's Mountain, Albemarle County, which he farmed as quarters. He was never a resident of Albemarle County but lived instead in Charles City County at his home, Shirley.

The road ordered opened in 1734 to Carter's quarter soon acquired the name "Secretary's Road". Initially, the primary purpose of the road was to roll hogsheads of tobacco to the James River for shipment to market, a use which resulted in a name occasionally seen - the Secretary's Old Rolling Road.

On 21 January 1734 (O.S.), soon after the road was opened, the Justices of the Court ordered the Secretary's Road to be "esteemed no Publick Road".[2] This move was perhaps indicative of the influence of Secretary Carter. Although no specific order survives that reverses this designation, it is clear from the records

APPENDIX C

Description of Architectural Patterns Emerging Along the Road

PATTERN IN ARCHITECTURE

In the discussion of architectural pattern associated with the Secretary's Road, the notion of "pattern" must be broken down into two distinct components. Those relationships which exist between the characteristics internal to the buildings themselves might be referred to as "artifactual pattern". The manner in which these "artifacts" or buildings relate to their environment, and to each other, may be termed "contextual pattern".

An examination of the architecture situated along the route of the Secretary's Road reveals similarities between the internal characteristics of certain buildings. Some of these similarities concern the technology employed in construction, while others relate to the arrangement of spaces and fenestration.

One interesting and obviously discernible pattern concerning technology is the relationship between wealth and the selection of building materials. Monticello, Tufton, Morven, Ernscliff, Ellerslie, and Redlands are the structures within the bounds of this survey which employ brick as their primary building material. Certainly the availability of clay has some bearing on the frequent use of brick in the area. It is significant, however, that all of these houses were once the seats of substantial estates. The more modest dwellings on the survey are built consistently of wood. Chronology apparently has little to do with this phenomenon, as the use of brick stretches...

APPENDIX D

Building Types

Buildings surveyed thus far range from such formal ones as Bremo
(see Figure 9) built c. 1818 by John Hartwell Cocke to very humble,
dilapidated ones as the Brown-Parrott House (see Figure AI) of c. 1780.
Some houses, such as the Jeffersonian one (see Figure A2) of c. 1830 on
Cream Street in Charlottesville, were razed within a short time of
completion of the measured drawings.

Several house types seem to emerge. One such type is that of Castle
Hill (see Figure A3) where the frame portion was built in 1765 and in
1824 a brick addition was built parallel to it and facing the opposite
direction. The two buildings then were connected with a smaller portion
of building in the space between, thus forming an H shape in plan and
thus retaining the integrity of each building phase. Another type is that
of Limestone (see Figure A4), which was owned by James Monroe and where
his brother Andrew resided. Here, arranged along a longitudinal axis, the
lower side wings are eighteenth century and the middle columned portion
was added in 1828. Spring Hill (see Figure A5) is another example
typifying the longitudinal arrangement; this time a frame gable-roofed
house of the late eighteenth century to which a brick addition was added
in the early nineteenth century. One could learn much from these examples
when adding to old buildings today. Other similarities occur when one
house is the mirror image of another, such as the 1899 Supervisor's House
(see Figure A6) of the Alberene Soapstone Company and that of Crestwood,
(see Figure A7) of the same period, but located along the Three Notch'd
Road.

Some houses have been so drastically altered over the years that
only a careful investigation can determine their original date. Oaklands
(see Figure A8) dates from c. 1840 and burned in 1916. The house was then
converted to the popular bungalow style. The Shadows (see Figure A9) was
an early nineteenth century vernacular farm building which received
several Colonial Revival additions over the years.

Churches, such as the Buck Mountain Episcopal Church (see Figure
AIO) of 1749 and the Bremo Slave Chapel (see Figure All) of 1835,
constitute a considerable number of buildings along the roads. But
perhaps the most road-oriented building type is the tavern, of which many
eighteenth century examples still exist, including the D. S. Tavern (see
Figure A12) of 1740 and Nathaniel Burnley's Tavern (see Figure A13), of
the same date and relocated to its present site early in this century.

On the 1875 Peyton map of Albemarle County, sixty-four mills are
identified. Today only seven remain, none maintain their original use,
and only one is occupied with an adaptive use. One such mill identified
is the Merrie Mill (see Figure A14) of c. 1735.

It might be noted that one of the hazards, or pleasures, as the case might be, of the course is evidenced by the fact that one student surveyor purchased the **c.** 1790 Jarman-Harris miller's house (see Figure A15) along his survey portion of the Three Notch'd Road.

Other buildings include vernacular examples, such as the log saddlebag one of the Wakefield Slave Quarters (see Figure A1S) **of c.** 1781 and the barn (see Figure A17) at Bremo of **c.** 1816 with its fieldstone columns, cupola with a bell that was a gift from Lafayette, and a sundial clock. For a vernacular typology, this barn is perhaps the only "classical" one in America.

Other readily recognizable national landmarks are also eighteenth century road oriented; for example, Jefferson's 1825 Rotunda (see Figure A18) is located at the University of Virginia along the Three Notch'd Road, as is the home, Monticello, (see Figure A19) of 1770-1809 located at the intersection of that road and the Secretary's Road. It is shown here in both its present and pre-1789 version.

Figure A1.   Brown-Parrott house, Albemarle County
Virginia, c. 1780.

Figure A2.   Jeffersonian house on Cream Street,
Charlottesville, Virginia, c. 1830.

Figure A3.   Castle Hill, Albemarle County,
             Virginia, 1765, 1824.

Figure A4. Limestone, Albemarle County, Virginia, 18C, 1828.

Figure A5. Spring Hill, Albemarle County, Virginia, late 18C, early 19C.

Figure A6.   Supervisor's house, Alberene,
            Albermarle County, Virginia, 1899.

Figure A7.   Crestwood, Albemarle County,
Virginia, c. 1890.

Figure A8.   Oaklands, Albemarle County, Virginia,
c. 1840 and after 1916.

Figure A9.   The Shadows, Albemarle County,
Virginia, early 19C and with
later additions.

Figure A10.   Buck Mountain Episcopal Church,
Albemarle County, Virginia, 1749.

Figure A11.   Bremo slave chapel, Fluvanna
County, Virginia, 1835.

Figure A12.   D. S. Tavern, Albemarle County, Virginia, 1740.

Figure A13.   Nathaniel Burnley's Tavern, Albemarle County, Virginia, 1740, 1780.

Figure A14. Merrie Mill, Albemarle
County, Virginia,
c. 1735.

Figure A15. Jarman-Harris Miller's house,
Albemarle County, Virignia,
c. 1790.

Figure A16.   Wakefield slave quarters,
Albemarle County, Virginia,
c. 1781.

Figure A17.   Bremo barn, Fluvanna County,
Virginia, c. 1816.

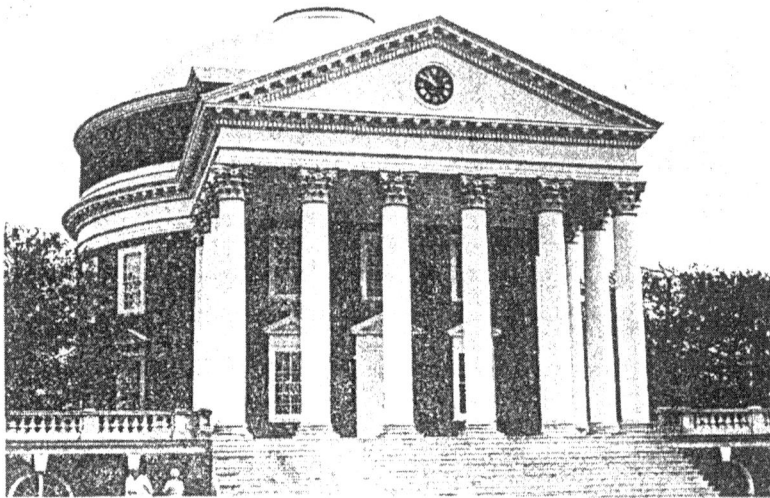

Figure A18.   Rotunda, University of Virginia,
               Albemarle County, Virginia, 1825.

Figure A19. Monticello, Albemarle County, Virginia, pre-1789 version and 1809 alteration.

INDEX

www.ingramcontent.com/pod-product-compliance
Lightning Source LLC
Chambersburg PA
CBHW050716100426

42735CB00041B/3325